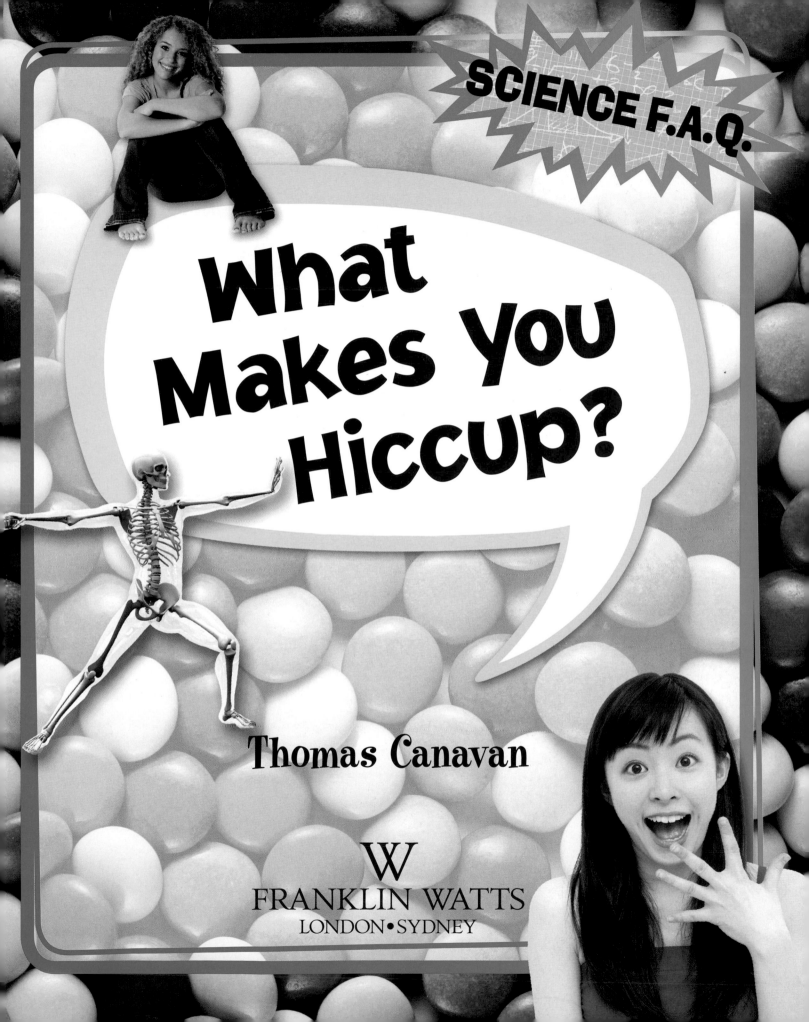

SCIENCE F.A.Q.

What Makes You Hiccup?

Thomas Canavan

W

FRANKLIN WATTS

LONDON • SYDNEY

First published in 2013 by Franklin Watts

Copyright © 2013 Arcturus Publishing Limited

Franklin Watts
338 Euston Road
London
NW1 3BH

Franklin Watts Australia
Level 17/207 Kent Street, Sydney, NSW 2000

Produced by Arcturus Publishing Limited,
26/27 Bickels Yard, 151–153 Bermondsey Street, London SE1 3HA

Editor: Joe Harris
Picture researchers: Annabel Stones and Joe Harris
Designer: Ian Winton

Picture credits: All images supplied by Shutterstock.

A CIP catalogue record for this book is available from the British Library.

Dewey Decimal Classification Number: 612

ISBN: 978 1 4451 2234 2

Franklin Watts is a division of Hachette Children's Books, an Hachette UK company.
www.hachette.co.uk

Printed in China

SL002661EN
Supplier 03, Date 0513 Print Run 2363

Contents

It's break time

It's time to bone up on those bits of you that sticks and stones can break. But how much do you really know about the job that your skeleton does?

Why don't you **laugh** when you hit your **funny bone?**

Because it hurts! And it hurts so much because you've just hit a nerve. Most nerves are protected by bone or muscle. But the ulnar nerve in your elbow is the largest unprotected nerve in your body. It's possible that the term 'funny bone' comes from the name of a nearby bone in your upper arm. That name – humerus – is like the word 'humorous', which means 'funny'.

Do you grow more bones as you get older?

No, you do just the opposite. Babies are born with more than 300 bones. Adults have 206 bones. The number goes down because bones join together to become bigger, stronger bones. And that starts to happen when you're about 12 years old.

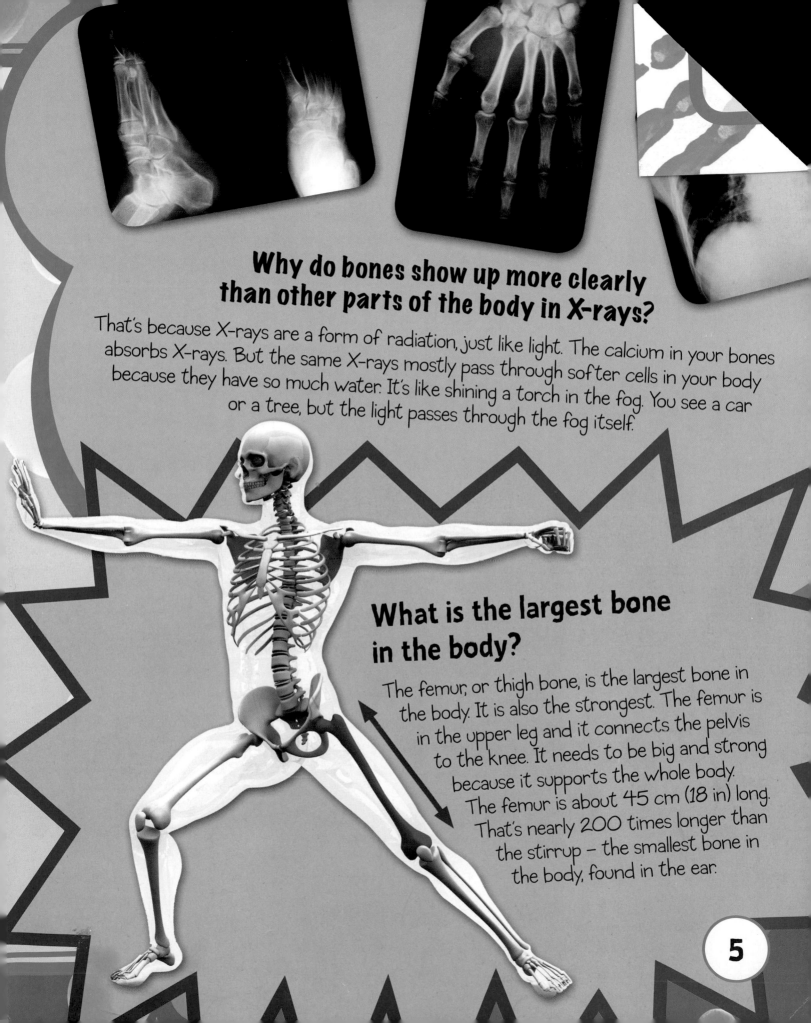

Why do bones show up more clearly than other parts of the body in X-rays?

That's because X-rays are a form of radiation, just like light. The calcium in your bones absorbs X-rays. But the same X-rays mostly pass through softer cells in your body because they have so much water. It's like shining a torch in the fog. You see a car or a tree, but the light passes through the fog itself.

What is the largest bone in the body?

The femur, or thigh bone, is the largest bone in the body. It is also the strongest. The femur is in the upper leg and it connects the pelvis to the knee. It needs to be big and strong because it supports the whole body. The femur is about 45 cm (18 in) long. That's nearly 200 times longer than the stirrup – the smallest bone in the body, found in the ear.

I beg your pardon

Atchoo! You know you should say 'excuse me' when you've made people turn and look at you... Now it's time to learn the reasons for what just happened!

HIC!

What makes you hiccup?

It's pretty easy to say what makes you hiccup. Usually you hiccup because something has irritated your tummy. And we know what a hiccup is. It's a sudden tightening of your breathing muscles. The 'hic' sounds when a piece of skin flaps shut over your windpipe. The real mystery is why you hiccup. Scientists still can't agree on that one.

Is yawning catching?

Yes it is, but no one is quite sure why. Human beings and chimpanzees are the only animals that yawn when they see another yawn. But it gets even stranger. Very small children don't yawn when someone near them does. As they get older, people seem to learn to do copycat yawning. So a single yawn can set a whole roomful of people off!

6

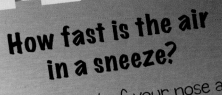

How fast is the air in a sneeze?

Air rushes out of your nose and mouth at more than 160 km/h (100 mph) when you sneeze. It's one of your body's ways of keeping your nose clear. Usually you have no control over whether you're going to sneeze. That's because it is a natural reflex and not something you can plan. A typical sneeze contains up to 40,000 tiny drops of liquid mixed in with the air.

How **loud** is the loudest **burp?**

A burp is a harmless way of getting rid of air or gas that you might have swallowed. Fizzy drinks often make you burp because they are full of gas. Normally you can control how the gas will be released. So you can keep things pretty quiet. The world record for the loudest burp is 107 decibels. That's as loud as a lawnmower running next to you.

Act your age

Growing up is a one-way street, and there's no going backwards! Of course, all the interesting stuff happens in between birth and death, so let's find out a bit more about what happens as you get older.

How do our bodies know when to stop growing?

Our bodies are programmed to stop growing because of messages in our genes. Young children have 'growth plates' at the ends of their long bones. These plates are made of soft material that grows. When children reach their late teens, their genes send out signals. These signals tell the body to make substances that seal the growth plates. This stops the bones from growing any more.

Do people's nails grow even after they have died?

No, they don't. But it might seem as though nails (and hair) grow because our eyes play tricks on us. In life, our flesh contains lots of water. When people die, their skin dries out and shrinks. As the soft bits lose water and shrivel, the hard bits stay the same length. So it looks as though they've grown. Creepy, eh?

Why can't boys grow beards?

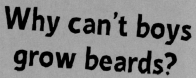

Your body uses chemicals called hormones to carry messages. A hormone called testosterone tells the face to grow hair. When a boy's body begins to change at puberty, the body starts to produce testosterone. This hormone leads to other changes such as a deeper voice and more muscles. Girls, like young boys, don't have the testosterone to create these changes.

Why do people live longer than they did in the past?

Most people in the UK can expect to live to about the age of 80. That's 30 years longer than in 1900. And it's more than 50 years longer than the average lifespan in Ancient Rome. We now have better food and medicine to fight disease. Plus people know how important it is to stay clean in order to stop the spread of germs.

Just be sensible

Your body uses all of its senses to 'make sense' of the world around you. How much sense do you think you can make from these questions?

Why can't you tickle yourself?

Scientists think that you laugh when you're tickled because you're a little bit scared. It's a way of letting off steam. The feeling of being tickled is like when a small insect crawls over you. You want to wriggle and maybe scream because you don't know what might happen. Similarly, your body is a little worried when someone surprises you with a tickle. But you can't surprise yourself – so you can't tickle yourself.

Why don't you taste things when you have a cold?

It's because two of your senses – taste and smell – are so closely linked. Although you may think you just taste food when you're eating, it's really a combination of both taste and smell. Your nose gets blocked when you have a cold, so you don't smell things well. If you can't smell what you're eating it's harder to get the full taste of it.

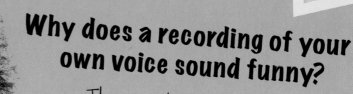

Why does a recording of your own voice sound funny?

The sound of your voice comes to you in two ways. One is through the air. The other is through the bones in your own body. You hear sounds coming through your bones as deeper than the 'air' sound. Normally the two combine in what you hear. But a recording of your voice picks up only the lighter, 'air' sound. To hear the deeper 'bone' sound, try speaking while wearing earplugs.

Why does pepper make you sneeze?

Your nose is designed to let only air pass through. It has three defences – small hairs in the nostrils, mucus... and sneezing. These defences either trap invaders or push them out. Dust and other tiny objects tickle the nerves in your nose and make you sneeze. But pepper contains a chemical that makes your nose nerves even more sensitive. So it has a greater chance of making you sneeze.

Pick up the pace

Being healthy is all about (pant, pant) being fit and knowing about (puff, puff) how your body works. Once you know a bit more about yourself, then you can pick up the pace and get even fitter.

Is there a limit to how fast athletes can run?

Top athletes today are much faster than runners of 100 or even 30 years ago. That's largely because of better food and improved training. There's probably a limit to how fast even the best athlete can go – but we still have many things to find out about what happens in the legs and feet when an athlete runs.

Why is it hard to walk uphill?

Simple really – it's all because of gravity. That's the force that draws everything towards the centre of the Earth. Gravity helps if you're walking or riding your bike downhill because it's pulling in the right direction. Going uphill, though, means working against the same force.

Does your weight vary during the day?

Most people weigh less first thing in the morning than at other times of day. It's mainly because of water. At night you lose a lot of water as you breathe out and sweat. Then you go to the toilet when you wake up. Getting rid of all of this water means you lose a bit of weight. During the day you drink again and your weight goes back up.

Why do some people count calories?

People gain or lose weight because of energy. Food energy is measured in calories. You gain calories when you eat. Exercise and normal body activities burn up energy. That energy is also measured in calories. So if you eat fewer calories than you burn off, then you lose weight.

60

450

25

300

Pass it on

How many times have you heard that you've got your dad's eyes or your grandma's curly hair? How do we end up being tall, or sporty, or left-handed?

Why are some people left-handed?

Whether you are left- or right-handed is partly controlled by your genes. It's also linked to human development over thousands of years. Scientists believe that being right-handed helped early humans build many skills, like writing. But left-handed people still had some advantages in fighting and hunting.

Which part of the world has the **tallest** people?

The tallest humans are among the groups of people living by the River Nile in East Africa. It is common to see men almost 2 m (6 ft, 8 in) tall. If you have tall parents you are quite likely to be tall too – although what you eat and your lifestyle are also important.

Can we inherit the ability to speak French or do difficult maths problems?

No one is born with the ability to speak a foreign language or to work out difficult sums. But people can inherit talents that make it easier for them to learn those skills. It's the same with sports. No one is born a footballer or tennis star. But some people find it easier to become good at these sports.

What is a test-tube baby?

Babies develop after a father's sperm cell joins with a mother's egg cell. Normally that happens in a tube inside the mother's body. Sometimes the tube is damaged and the sperm can't reach the egg. So scientists remove sperm cells and eggs to join them together in a test tube. The new unborn baby (the embryo) is put back inside the mother's womb to develop normally.

Eye eye, sir

Many people think that sight is the most important of all the senses. After all, we say 'I see' when we mean 'I understand'. Cast your eye over these questions to see what you understand about sight.

Why do onions make us cry?

Chemicals in onion oil (the moist bit) mix together when you cut into an onion. They create a new chemical – with a 21-letter name! This new chemical mixes with the air around it. It's this air that stings the glands near your eyes, and the glands produce tears in defence.

Are blind people's other senses super-strong?

No, they're not, but blind people often use their other senses better than most people. For example, blind people hear sounds in exactly the same way as other people. But they are usually much better at working out where those sounds are coming from.

Can special glasses help colour-blind people?

No, glasses really can't help. Glasses are designed to change the path of light coming into the eyes. That is very helpful if your eye cannot focus properly. But colour-blindness has to do with how the eye detects different types of light. Colour-blind people are missing some of the cells that tell the difference between colours.

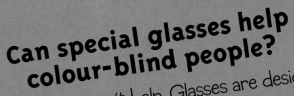

Why don't people all have the same colour eyes?

The colour of your eyes depends on the amount of melanin (a natural colouring) in your iris. That's the bit just outside the pupil, or 'bull's-eye' of the eye. Brown eyes come from having lots of melanin. Blue-eyed people have less. Melanin helps absorb harmful rays from the Sun. That's why people from hot regions often have brown eyes.

17

Food for thought

They say that some people live to eat and others eat to live. Which of those describes you? Think about it! In the meantime here are some questions to chew over.

Why does your tummy **rumble** when you're hungry?

Swallowed food passes through the stomach and into the intestines. Muscles squeeze and push the food along as it gets digested. But about two hours after your tummy's emptied, the brain sends a signal to start the squeezing and pushing again. You're probably hungry by that time. But squeezing and pushing those muscles around an empty tummy makes quite a noise.

RUMBLE RUMBLE

Does eating fish make you clever?

This advice seemed like a fairy story for many years. Now scientists believe it is true. People who eat some types of fish (such as tuna and mackerel) do score better on tests. These fish contain a fatty acid called Omega-3 that helps more blood flow to your brain.

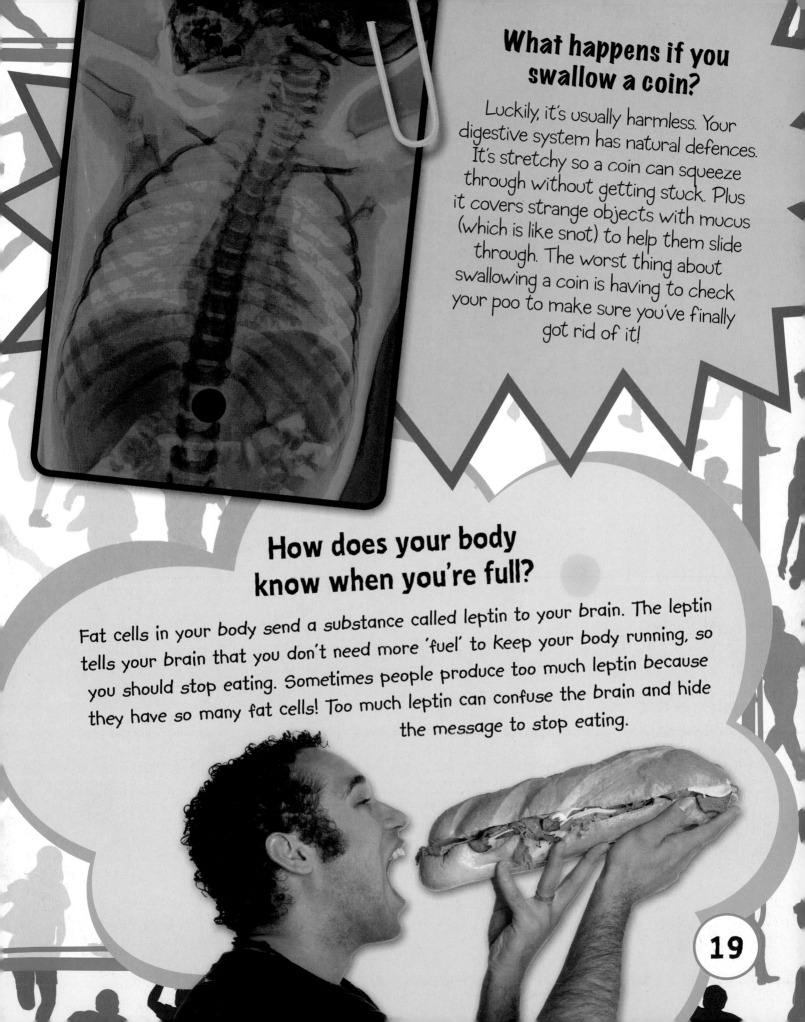

What happens if you swallow a coin?

Luckily, it's usually harmless. Your digestive system has natural defences. It's stretchy so a coin can squeeze through without getting stuck. Plus it covers strange objects with mucus (which is like snot) to help them slide through. The worst thing about swallowing a coin is having to check your poo to make sure you've finally got rid of it!

How does your body know when you're full?

Fat cells in your body send a substance called leptin to your brain. The leptin tells your brain that you don't need more 'fuel' to keep your body running, so you should stop eating. Sometimes people produce too much leptin because they have so many fat cells! Too much leptin can confuse the brain and hide the message to stop eating.

19

Sleep secrets

What happens when you're asleep? Do you dream, talk or even go for a walk? And how much sleep do you need? Read on to find out about the secrets of sleep.

Why do children have to go to bed before grown-ups?

Children need to go to bed earlier and get more sleep than adults for two reasons. One is to help the body build up its energy. Growing uses up lots of energy. The other is that sleep itself helps the brain. Scientists believe that a child's brain needs sleep to develop.

Why do we dream?

We all dream, even if we can't remember our dreams in the morning. But doctors can't agree why we dream. Some say that dreams have no real purpose. Others believe that they are a way of dealing with problems that trouble us when we're awake.

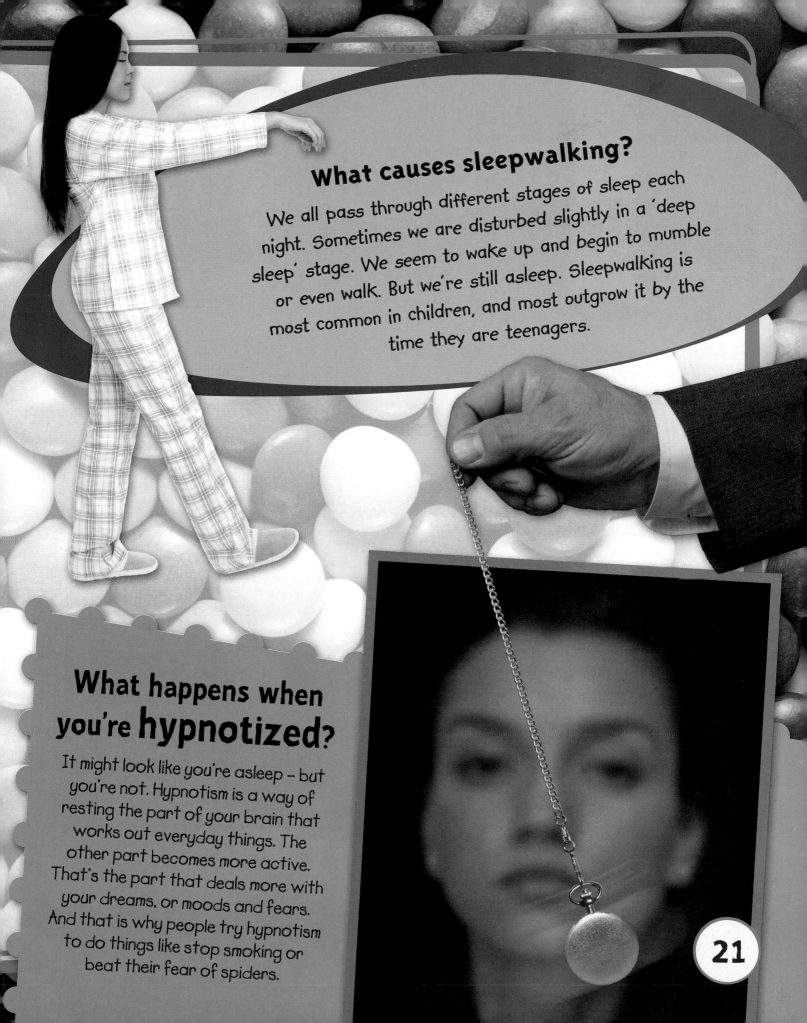

What causes sleepwalking?

We all pass through different stages of sleep each night. Sometimes we are disturbed slightly in a 'deep sleep' stage. We seem to wake up and begin to mumble or even walk. But we're still asleep. Sleepwalking is most common in children, and most outgrow it by the time they are teenagers.

What happens when you're hypnotized?

It might look like you're asleep – but you're not. Hypnotism is a way of resting the part of your brain that works out everyday things. The other part becomes more active. That's the part that deals more with your dreams, or moods and fears. And that is why people try hypnotism to do things like stop smoking or beat their fear of spiders.

21

Hair, there and everywhere

Do you spend ages thinking about your hair, or is it something that you're happy to cover with a hat? How would you look with a five-metre beard, or if you were bald?

How long could a beard grow?

A man's beard grows about 13 cm (5 in) a year. There's nothing to stop this growth unless he chooses to trim it. The man with the longest beard ever recorded was Hans Langseth of Norway. His beard was 5.65 m (18 ft, 6 in) long when he died.

Why do some people have curly hair?

You inherit your type of hair from your parents or grandparents just as you inherit hair or eye colour. The way your hair grows depends on the tubes on your head where they start off. These are called follicles. Hair coming out of a circular follicle grows straight. An oval-shaped follicle sets hair growing in curls.

Why do we have eyebrows?

Scientists believe that eyebrows developed to keep water and sweat from flowing into the eyes. It wouldn't be good to be wiping water away from your eyes if a wolf were chasing you. But eyebrows have another job, too. They send signals to other people about how you're feeling – happy, sad, cross or surprised.

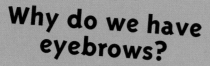

Why do some men go bald, but others don't?

It depends mainly on whether the men on either their mother's or father's side of the family were bald. The gene for baldness destroys the cells that produce hair. Poor diet and illness can also lead to baldness.

Skin deep

Your skin is your largest organ. It covers around two square metres and the outer layer is dead. Didn't know that? Read on for some more skin surprises.

Why do your hands **wrinkle** when they're wet?

Your skin contains a substance called keratin to keep it strong and moist. The skin surface has loads of dead keratin cells. In the bath these dead cells soak up more water than the live keratin cells beneath. The soaked-up outer layer then gets a little floppy because it has run out of lower layers to stick to. Your fingers and toes get most wrinkled because they have the thickest layers of skin.

What causes freckles?

The simple answer is – the Sun. Your skin produces a dark colouring called melanin to protect it from the Sun. Usually the melanin spreads out evenly to make a tan. Sometimes it can come out in blotches – freckles. People get freckles mainly on their face and arms because these are the areas that are most exposed to the Sun.

Why does sunburn make your skin peel?

Sunburn kills the layer of living skin cells below the outer layer of skin. But your body starts growing new cells to replace the dead bits. The dead layer stays in place to protect the new cells growing beneath. When the new layer is ready, the dead outer layer peels away.

Why do people have different skin colours?

Like freckles, skin colour depends on melanin. Melanin protects the skin from the harmful effects of the Sun. People in hot, sunny places, such as Africa, need more protection than people in cooler places. That's why their skin is naturally darker. But sunlight also helps us to make vitamins. People in places with weaker sunlight have lighter skin because that skin colour helps the sunlight to sink in.

25

on't feel well

When your body is under attack from germs and infections it has lots of ways of fighting back. Sometimes, though, it needs a bit of help from modern medicine to fight off a disease...

Why do you 'run a temperature' when you are unwell?

Your body gets warmer when it is fighting an infection. This warming up is called a fever. When it detects an infection, your body produces chemicals called pyrogens. The blood takes the pyrogens to the brain. The brain then 'turns up the heat' in order to kill off the germs that are causing the infection.

Why does your nose run in cold weather?

Your nose checks on the air heading down to your lungs. It usually produces mucus to push dust and other bits out of your air passages. Tiny blood vessels in your nostrils become wider in cold weather to warm the air. But the extra blood also makes the nose pump out more mucus, giving you a runny nose.

Why do people get seasick?

Your brain receives signals from other parts of the body. They tell the brain whether you're moving or not. The signal for balance comes from inside your ear. On a rough sea it tells your brain that you're going up and down. But your eyes see that the tables and walls on the ship aren't moving. Your brain gets confused and the result is that awful feeling of seasickness.

What was the Black Death?

It was a disease that doctors now call the bubonic plague. Between 1348 and 1350 it swept across Asia and Europe. Millions of people died, including up to half of all Europeans. The disease was spread by fleas. Victims got horrible blisters that turned black. Modern medicine can treat the disease, but people in the Middle Ages usually died if they got it.

Anybody's guess

You've got a lifetime ahead of you to learn more about the marvels of the human body. Here are a few intriguing questions to get you started.

Why do you have a belly button?

You developed inside your mother before you were born. For nine months you got all the food and oxygen you needed through a tube that went into your tummy. But once you were born you could use your mouth and nose to eat and breathe. So the doctor tied a knot in the tube and snipped it. This knot is your belly button.

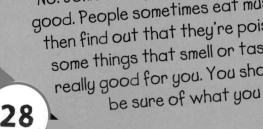

Does poison always taste bad?

No. Sometimes poisonous things can taste good. People sometimes eat mushrooms and then find out that they're poisonous. And some things that smell or taste bad are really good for you. You should always be sure of what you eat.

Do right-handed people also prefer using their right foot?

Usually they do, but not always. About 80 per cent of right-handers prefer using their right foot. Left-handers are a little different. About half of them prefer using their right foot.

What causes goose-bumps?

It all comes from a time when humans were covered with much more hair. And it's still true with furry animals. When it's cold, the body fluffs out the hair or fur to make it into a better blanket. Even though the hair on our arms is thin and wispy, it still fluffs out. And the skin doing the pushing forms 'goose-bumps'.

Glossary

air passage One of the tubes that lets air pass from the nose down into the lungs.

calcium A chemical that makes your bones strong.

decibel A unit of measurement to compare sound levels.

embryo An animal (including humans) developing inside its mother at the first stages of growth.

gene A combination of chemicals that signals how an animal will develop.

gland An organ that produces hormones and other substances to fight disease.

gravity The force that draws objects towards each other.

hormone A chemical that acts as a messenger in the body.

infection An illness caused by an outside object attacking the body.

inherit To receive information about development from a parent's genes.

intestine One of the tubes extending from the stomach, to help digest food and get rid of waste.

irritate To hurt by touching or rubbing constantly.

melanin A dark substance produced by the body to protect the skin from the worst effects of the Sun.

mucus A slimy liquid that the body produces to protect and moisten.

nerve Part of the network of tissues that send signals from one part of the body to another.

puberty The period in the early teens when children begin to mature into adults.

radiation The process of sending off waves of energy.

reflex An automatic movement by the body to protect it.

skeleton The set of bones that gives shape and support to the body.

sperm A cell produced by a male, which mixes with the female egg to produce a baby.

test tube A narrow glass tube used in science experiments.

vitamin A substance that the body can't produce but which is necessary in small quantities for health.

windpipe A tube-like passage that allows air to pass from the throat to the lungs.

womb A hollow organ in the female body where embryos develop into babies ready to be born.

Further Reading

Body Science by DK Publishing (DK Books, 2009)

First Encyclopedia of the Human Body by Fiona Chandler (Usborne Publishing, 2011)

The Human Body by Peter Riley (Franklin Watts, 2009)

Kingfisher Readers: Human Body by Anita Ganeri (Kingfisher, 2013)

Project X Journeys: Human Body Adventures by Alison Blank (OUP Oxford, 2009)

Your Senses by Sally Morgan (Collins Educational, 2012)

Websites

BBC – KS2 Bitesize
www.bbc.co.uk/bitesize/ks2/science/living_things/
The excellent BBC Bitesize 'Living Things' section has a number of interactive areas devoted to the human body and health.

The Haunted House, How Does Your Body Move?
www.bonesandharry.co.uk/
The site is an interactive journey to learn about the bones that make up the human skeleton and how they move.

The Heart: An Online Investigation
www.fi.edu/learn/heart/index.html
The renowned Franklin Institute's site lets you explore the heart and circulatory system by following blood through the blood vessels.

The Human Body Cyberhunt
http://icteachers.co.uk/children/cyberhunts/human_body/body.htm
You can answer important questions about the human body, then use links to find specialist sites providing the answers in each case.

Your senses – eyes and seeing
http://lincs.skoool.co.uk/content/primary/science/eyes_and_seeing/index.html
Interactive drag-and-drop activities will guide you through an examination of all aspects of human sight.

Index

Series contents

SCIENCE F.A.Q.

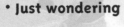

Do Plants Really Eat Insects? • It's a jungle out there! • Try this for size • Peckish plants • Jobs to do • Birds and bees... and trees • Peculiar plants • Changing nature • Going to extremes • Get a life! • Power plants • Eat your greens! • Don't be so wet! • Just wondering

Does It Really Rain Frogs? • Home sweet globe • Stormy weather • Round and round • The right impression • A large shake, please • Forcing the issue • Just give me some time • Lighten up • Making a splash • Rain, rain, go away • Now you've done it • Going to extremes • Air we go

What Makes You Hiccup? • It's break time • I beg your pardon • Act your age • Just be sensible • Pick up the pace • Pass it on • Eye eye, sir • Food for thought • Sleep secrets • Hair, there and everywhere • Skin deep • I don't feel well • Anybody's guess

Why Are Black Holes Black? • Sunny side up • Meet the neighbours • Hey — lighten up! • Over the moon • Up, up and away • Here comes trouble • Sky-high science • Goin' my way? • Tighten your space helmet • Heavens above • Long ago and far away... • That's life! • It's out of this world

Why Do Ice Cubes Float? • Food for thought • Now for some hard questions • It's only natural • It all boils down to science • Pass the gas • Read all about it • Whatever floats your boat • Water wonders • Are you stuck? • That's really cool! • Metal workout • Changing things • Still stumped?

Why Do Zebras Have Stripes? • Going for the record • What you see is what you get • All at sea? • Come to your senses • Jurassic park life • Creepy crawlies • Yackety-yak • Baby beasties • What's for dinner? • Up and away • Fact or fiction? • Just like us? • It's round-up time